I0538538

Nothing.
No One.
Nowhere.

Volume 2 ~ Number I
Virgogray Press ~ 2015

Edited by Michael Aaron Casares
Cover art- "Georgia Viaduct Entrance, Vancouver B.C." by Allen Forrest
Magazine design by Michael Aaron Casares
More information at www.nothingnoonenowhere.com

Nothing. No One. Nowhere.
Vol. 2 No. 1. September, 2015
ISSN: 2158-1223
ISBN: 978-0692519486

Published by Virgogray Press

Nothing. No One.

Nowhere.

Table of Contents

Poetry

Short Fiction

Artwork

Breakfast in Bed

Pancakes from the sky
with maple syrup heaven
drip down in waves,
covering the empty plate with salvation
of vitamins and passion

Sugar high junkie fever
pours from the sun in spades
as a knife in the side
to the guts
to the heart
where a furnace burns
in fiery heat, seeking solace
but no comfort comes...
so we eat more and then more
until the stomach expands
with elasticity of taste bud frenzy

Insatiable with lust
as the prism penis protrudes
A missile looking for a well —
somewhere to reside in paradise
where wisdom lacks not
and red blood finds release
out the pores in sweat
between the sheets
with sweet expulsion

The candy embrace lasts but a moment
and then the day must begin...
we can not lay here forever
drowning in butter

Swept Away By the Sands of Innocent Ruminations

Ignorance abounds
until innocence is snuffed
out like a flame
after the moth takes a hit
directly to the soul
A fire in the distance
crashes across vibrational fields
from the sun
to the spirit
in a split second
shattering the sins
of one million disembodied
cancerous tumors
during their death march
across the entropic void

Mind numbed and atrophied
in vomited nihilism
as the fear contagiously spreads
in a new wave
Albatross crash landing
with a broken millstone
hung around the twisted neck
of a tattered tantrum
running amok
beneath the low-hanging fruit
which offers its comfort
to those who are lost
in the bottom of a hole
dug for the long sweet dirt nap

Golden casket lining
the just rewards
of a planet in sharp decline
with direct correlation
to collective consciousness
going nuts over failed fantasies
Illusions in the background
cater to the absolute
madness of a symphony

from the far flung stars
raining a musical cacophony
into the ear wax plugs
of a drum getting smashed

Twilight of the hammer
coming across the face
of fallen false idols
Cracking the rib
coating the ash with dust
to create a new feeling
in the garden of emotional drainage
where all is lost
to the ages of decimation

Apocalyptic Fervor
takes it cue
from the crowd
sourced by fiat frenzy
into a pyramid of pulsating
triangulated rhythms
Sucking on the stocks
seeking out a market
to fleece the sheep
to ruin the rube
to mark the Beast
on its forehead
with a bounty of confusion

Crystallized in purity
as a rarified form of diluted oxygen
sucked dry atop the mountain peak
in a final gasp
before taking the plunge
down the rabbit's hole
in a never ending journey
across tangent meandering interludes
through the psychedelic psyche
of a hypnotic trance
to the ninth realm and back
before the dream even truly begins

Pineal calcification
corrupts the inner dimension
and we weep for the fault lines
as they fracture
beneath the once proud city
now lying in ruins
like Atlantis
version 2.0
toppled once more
in the vicious cycle

This Is My City

Through the my eyes,
my coffee and my smoke,
this is my city,
it belongs to me
like my arm
or like my mouth,
these are my lights,
my people, my problems,
my lives to judge and to
frown upon and to
play Hamlet or William Tell,
this is my wind
and my leaves
and my strange song
that my keyboard sings,
there are my wings,
mutilated and stuffed
into a green jar
in the basement of
a Russian hacker
with 20 kilos of fat
hanging from his belly,
those are my letters,
all 27 of them,
this is the city
that is rulled by chaos
and chance,
this is the world
thst frowns to me
like and old woman,
breaking a chiken's neck
with her bare hands,
these are my hands
and my sinner lips,
this is all I'll ever be,
stuffed in 100 words,
from a cafe in Leon city,
watching the moon
under a white
lamp.

The Romantic

"Shelley is greater than Keats," David insisted to his friend Walker, who was by now only pretending to pay attention to this grad school argument. They'd each taken a solid hit of windowpane acid that was starting to kick in.

"Keats," Walker muttered, wondering if he really should have also swallowed the lude just to take the edge off.

"Unacknowledged legislator and all that..." but David was starting to drift.

"Bright star...I hold it towards you..." Walker was also losing interest. He leaned back in the bean bag chair just before the floor turned to spiders and wondered if he would ever truly love.

He looked ok, he knew that, handsome, gray eyes, black hair. He saw how they looked at him, his Thursday tutees--the chesty Jewish girl who loved Neruda, the skinny red-headed gay guy headed for a Tony.

Of course he didn't flirt back. He was the tutor.

Twelve hours later, there were no longer scorpions on the ceiling and if he closed his eyes he no longer saw flaming auras on his hands and feet. The good part of the trip was over too. Walker rinsed his mouth, washed his face, and struggled into the light of day--late afternoon April.

There was something terribly wrong with Harvard Square, but he couldn't place it, until he realized...silence. No cars, no horns, no panhandlers, no pedestrians, no...students.

He caught the whiff of tear gas just as he saw the shadow of the cop's stick aim for his skull.

He jerked, ducked, and took off running, even though the baton had connected with his ear, a pain worse than anything he had ever experienced. It was bleeding copiously. And he ran, as if he were in prime condition rather than an occasional ping pong player.

At last, a corner, an alley, and heavenly sight, Passim's Cafe. The door barred. Two Pre-Raphaelite girls standing guard, one on each side of the espresso machine, ready to face down the pigs.

Of course, they rushed to let him in. He never did know the name of the taller beautiful one. The sweet-faced brown haired girl was named Laurel, but he didn't know that yet. Nor that in six months they'd be engaged and she'd give him a life time of devotion, competent children, the interest of her career, and half the profits from a small but productive farm in Nebraska.

He slid to the floor, bleeding, and his head landed in her lap. He looked up at her.

"who is the greater poet, Shelley or Keats?" he asked.

"Keats," she said. "I'm a botany major but I'm going for Keats."

"Good," he said as he blacked-out in her arms.

Beyond X-Ray Blindness

ghostwritten rules engulfing

euphoric
mind-sets
thriving &

oppressing
behind tilted cyber ideal-shields
swarming onto networking sites
doused with altruistic armor and
diversionary overloads reradiated
while constantly sedated forward

5-0 Sunlamp

    Peep shows

                    everywhere
nitespot ooze

               backstage
               interviewing
               after hour
               consumers
commenting on screams inside
glittering karaoke machines full
of old red cough drops and gum

Connected Theories or How The Body Becomes an Explorer of Exterior Confinements

Each dotted ambush of light
wrote chaos against clarity's
usual delineation of meaning.

    Hands and stone held
    dancing flames, partitioned
    by cold and damp imposition.

When irony is explained it
relocates the tongue to the
back of the mouth's comfortable
projection. Nothing

        extends beyond a mirror's peripheral
        collaboration of angles and grayed
        foggy exterior legends—

margin notes, an expected fragility
of a tomorrow's version of learned
behavior.

From Memory III

Glass broke toward this morning's earliest avalanche of silence. Angled language trampolines, inward/out upon stammering rain and spatial spiral-dancing echoes. I wore words, spelled clothing using hands and divided hours in replicating synonyms, elasticized interrogations. Each promise lost voice. Each turning emblem sunk and wore dimming light like a breath simmering into water's open experience.

I couldn't fathom. An eye closed and halved a timid way back home. A recalled scent threw its tongue onto the whole pant of my whispering. Colors saw their distancing ghosts, an aged version of pale splaying crayon. Something said: a misery is function of behavior's typical communication. I said: your truant belief is a body of controlling hyper multilayers and inborn feelings of philosophical dementia.

8:00 a.m. I humbled my legs and ran to the crow cradling affluence of tone and partition. Blur. Timid, the higher hours of this morning hid until against my feet shrouded within comfort and pain's best altering dimension. Noon climbed. An exterior of sudden discomfort cried an ache, an aching entrance to the ear's rest and unobstructed healing.

After Midnight

After midnight,
message from a former love
twenty years or more--
he still thinks of me every New Year's Eve,
still calls me "Chief"
I smile from the memories;
nights out dancing and drinking,
watching the moonlight sidle over the pond,
navigating 'round that gear shift
in his '78 Supra.

Tonight my husband reaps benefits
of young love's remembrance.

As Waves Crash

as waves crash against the rocky shore
I throw myself against you
to soften your rough edges
fit myself in your craggy spaces,
wrap my life with yours

at times gently caressing you.
other times, in full fury, with all the powers
I can summon from King Triton, Poseidon,
all the sea dragons of lore,
I crash, flooding your shore,
beating my fists
against you to break you
to make you be with me
never understanding
you are stone
and I am sea

Sahara

We are on opposite ends of a sandstorm
and the wind is our love.

Stained Madonna

I move your hands along my torso
like watercolors across stone.
They leave their scattered mark
and my tears are temporary.
Touch me with fingers of molten ash,
harbor your woe in my flesh.
I never have enough of never bearing
my own grief; let me taste yours.
If you were a glass madonna
I would take you under a bridge,
say holy prayers, holy prayers,
then smash you on the concrete bricks.

The Wino Saul

The beggar was reading his begging sign
as if it was the Bible
and I wondered, "Is that the Bible in his lap
written on cardboard, condensed to
the essential strokes and slashes of humanity?"
And when I turned to look again,
he raised it up: *Blinded for life.*
Anything helps.

I Like The Label Smoker / You Can Smell Me Burning

I have (too many)
untitled thoughts
because
I have trouble with labels.

I have trouble;
it hides
behind the titles
I don't give to [things].
Admittedly,
I say, I am a smoker.
I've heard
It's a trendy way to kill yourself.

slowly,
choking on smoke rings,
inhaling and holding,
I only have the lungs
to hold things

that disappear
when I let them go.

I cannot name this burning.
I wouldn't use my tongue to describe to you
the taste of dying.

But I know you can smell it,
the decay in my clouded breath,
the fire in my tarred chest.

When you find my scent
in the wind
I hope you will name it
Name it after my ashes.

Puppeteering in Third Person

She wakes up another morning.
Consciousness is her less helpless struggle.
She begins poems this way
so readers know
how to tread her synaptic puzzle.

Her mind,
a funhouse-mirrored labyrinth
reflecting self-doubt
and unreasonable expectations.
"No big deal", she convinces
these warped images.
"haha" she will flippantly tag
to the end of her text messages.

She battles romanticized versions of self.
The self she dressed up for this morning.
But who can everyone else see?

A basket of masks sits in a grab bag by the door,
beckoning.
Near her boots worn to empower her.
Maybe sneakers.
Sneakers are worn more comfortably
on other peoples' eyes.
She chooses slippers.
She won't leave the house today.

Festival patrons,
her circumstantial audience,
wear their lensless glasses.
She is just the spectacle.

Welcome to the game,
they will utter behind smug smiles.
Are they being smug?
Are they anything?
Are they thinking anything?
"You think too much,"
she says silently,

chuckling,
hoping everyone hears.

Endless apologies spew,
Coated in bile,
No one hears
there is empty.
Like a holey sock in her snowboot.
Know one knows.
And this makes her uncomfortable.
She is uncomfortable being alive
in a shell:
an armored vehicle of limbs
protecting such vital
explosions.

She lives in (too much) institution.
Under-pressure-cooking-kettle,
ticking-tea-timer,
She is mariennetted into
a life-size corporate puppet
hanging noosely
in a mom and pop shop.

She has an ache in the part of her brain
  which makes her heart work.
She has an ache in this part of the brain
  which hurts more doused in alcohol.
She has to write this poem in third person
  because it is less real.
She has to write this poem in third person
  because "she" could be any one of many "shes"
She has to write this poem in the third person
  because the first person is the last person
  she ever wanted to be.

It is always easier
to see herself when she's beside herselves.
Looking to these masked puppet walls.
The flimsy cardboard,
The floppy disc mind,
The unbearably barren chest cavity.

There is no wrong way to be, but
She and I...We
are just desperately needing
to perform the right one.

Much Needed Marginality

Looking through old notebooks I found
I write the word needed in the margins.

The first attempt at college,
I stopped writing in print and
switched to cursive indefinitely.

I needed to,
I needed a change.

The word needed flows across the page effortlessly,

it spins in ellipses
optically entrancing,
smooth to the touch

I don't know why I have needed
to write needed in my margins

I don't know what I was looking for.
I'm not sure if my confusion is my wonder
dizzying my orbit
So I could figure out where I needed to be going.

The scripted surface of page skin
bleeds a word that often lacks in
my writing

it's only in my margins
it's only on the outside
plaguing mindless scribble

I don't know if I write in oblong
circular motions because
thoughts spin and
ink spills out of hand
accidentally.

I write needed in the margins;
a subconscious doodle in a
boring class.

I have been writing needed
because I needed to feel something smooth,
something missing.

A page with the word scrawled across
it a dozen times,
calling for you
by name.

The Brightness

Your kiss wasn't magic
like the touch of a ghost:
serene and glorious,
or deep to the soul.
My love reached broader
across the straights and seas,
but I could not kiss you
like the face of dawn.
Instead, I called you
the brightness.

Trapped

Rose stood in the kitchen, in complete and utter shock, a blush of red rising on her left cheek. Frank stood in front of her, eyes wide in disbelief as he lowered his hand. She refused to cry, and stared at him, completely indifferent to everything around her. His chest was heaving from the heat of getting into the argument, and he could hear his heart pounding in his ears.

"Rosie, oh damn it," he gushed, "Rosie, I am so sorry, please forgive me." His eyes searched hers, looking for some kind of tender softening, but they were impassive. She shook her head slightly and shrugged her shoulders, brushing past him to get a cloth and some ice. Her daughter, Susan's artwork was still in the middle of the table, and there was an accidental line of oil paint across her self-portrait. She straightened the canvas as she walked towards the fridge.

Frank kept pleading with her as she moved about the house, gathering her ice pack together and sitting on the couch, staring blankly at the wall.
"Come on, Rose, you know I never meant to hurt you," he said and she gave a derisive laugh.
"You know, Frank, when we first started dating I might have actually believed that to be true. I thought that you would do anything or be anything simply to make sure that I was happy and knew I was loved. But then time passed and we weren't dewey eyed over each other anymore; still in love maybe, but not sickeningly so. We got hitched and then we got pregnant, and I could see the stress mounting on your shoulders. When you first started to nit-pick everything I did, I let it roll right off. It was just stress I reasoned," she said, removing the pack from her cheek to reposition the ice. "We moved to this house because we wanted a big backyard for Susie. Those few times when you came home with flowers, I fell in love all over again. But I shouldn't have caved, because soon I was your doormat. Every day you walked into the house, you walked over me as a greeting, and I welcomed you in —"

"Wait a minute," he cut in, hackles rising, but she shook her head.

"I had no idea how bad it had gotten until your siblings started to talk to me about us when you weren't around. They were shocked, they had never seen you this way before, couldn't believe their own eyes. But I was a good wife, I made the excuses and told them how much I still loved you...yada yada," she said, and a small giggle rose from her throat. Frank shoved her, hard. "For the longest time, I was waiting for you to break, you know, come unhinged. I had told them you would never hit me," she smiled. "Isn't that funny, Frank?"

She watched as the blue vein traveling up the side of his head throbbed, and she wasn't the least bit surprised when he blew, fist connecting first with her face, then her stomach. This time she did not hold back a few yelps of pain.

Susan came running down the stairs at the sound of her mother's cries and began screaming at her father. She launched herself onto Frank's back, but he broke her grasp easily, flinging her onto the floor. Her head hit the coffee table as she went down, and tore a bloody gash across the side of her face.

Rose's arms tried to subdue Frank, but they were feeble against his two hundred pound mass. When he was done, she looked up and saw a few tears trickling down his cheek. She was dumbfounded, what did he have to cry for?

"I'm sorry," he whispered, and then he left, the door clicking shut behind him.

There were small sobs from the floor. "Susan," she murmured, "sweetie, are you all right?"

Her daughter sat up slowly, pressing her hand against the cut on her head. "Will you leave him now? He's finally done it," she cried, "he's hurt both of us. I want us to leave him.

Please, Mom."

At that, Rose began to cry. "I didn't want him to hurt you. You should have stayed out of it," she whispered.

Susan shook her head. "I'll call 911." Her voice was unsteady when she had finally dialed, "I need someone to come to 94 Sherman Road, my father just beat my mother." She reached over and grabbed her mother's hand as she explained, and they waited in silence until there was a knock on the door. She answered it, and the police came in, followed quickly by members of EMS. They cleaned up her forehead and assessed her mother before placing Rose on a board. They all clambered into the ambulance. Her mother had a ruptured spleen.

Rose was numb to whatever happened after that. The doctors stitched her up and the police asked her questions while she was staying in the hospital. After four days they sent her home, and she had the locks changed. Susan helped her pack Frank's things in a box and set them out on the porch for him to take. When she and Susan were finally free of it all, they went upstairs and laid down on Rose's bed, watched TV and drank their way through four bottles of Gatorade and a package of vanilla cream wafers.

"Mom," Susan murmured, and Rose looked at her with a brow furrowed. "Was Dad ever nice to you?"

Rose let out a huff of breath, "Yeah, at one time, he was really sweet. I did marry him you know," she said, giving a small smile. "When we were around your age, we traveled the world and put locks in every popular city we could, claiming our love was eternal and all that bologna. The pictures are probably in a box in the attic somewhere. But we used to do normal things too, like mudding, going to the movies, bowling, the things young couples should do."

Susan snuggled into her mother's side, wrapping her arm around her. "What was he like back then?"

She had to think about it for a minute, her memory was getting to be foggy where it concerned Frank. "He was so funny and innocent. Sometimes he would say the most ridiculous things and when I started laughing he would duck his head and smile. Frank used to be really gentle too. When we would hold hands, he would make these little tickling circles on my skin."

She did it on Susan's hand and she started giggling.

There were a couple "tings" against the screen and Rose was distracted. There was a wasp buzzing in the corner of the window, hitting the glass constantly, confused by the entrapment.

"It's weird, but I can't really remember any of the good things I used to think about him," Susan said, breaking Rose's concentration. "For a while, I've been praying that he would lash out, just so you'd see what he really was. I didn't expect that doing my artwork would send him over the edge. I had to get it done for class," she broke off, stifling a sob," maybe if I had just gone to the studio at school he wouldn't have hurt you so bad…"

"No, Susie," Rose whispered. "He wasn't really angry about you doing your artwork. I think it was the stupid things that set him off...the dirty dishes in the sink from the night before...the fender-bender I got into last week...the bills. They were things he never talked about and the stress just kept mounting and mounting. The only person he ever takes it out on is me, I'm his punching bag. I provoked him to start hitting me all over again. I basically told him he was a douchebag."

"Among other things," Susan sniffled. They both started to laugh a little bit. "Can I sleep on Dad's side tonight, Mom?"

"Yeah, I don't think I'm ready to sleep alone," she admitted.

The doorbell rang. Susan ran down the stairs. There was silence. "Who is it, honey?"

Rose called down. Still nothing. Her hand gripped the railing as she walked down the stairs.

When Frank caught sight of her through the window, he began pounding on the door, yelling profanities. Their daughter was already in the living room, dialing the phone. Rose kept shaking her head, a tear clutching to her eyelid. She grabbed Susan and they hurried into the kitchen. The pounding stopped. Minutes later, there were blows against the window. The glass broke and shattered against the floor. As he fumbled for the lock, sirens sounded at the end of the street.

He had just gotten the door open when the cruisers pulled up.

"Frank," a policeman's voice came over a speakerphone, "put down the tire iron and step away from the door." Metal clanged on the wooden boards of the porch, and both of them crept quietly within view of the door. Police officers were apprehending Frank, and leading him into a cruiser. Another officer approached the door and knocked. He ensured both of them were not harmed and explained that Frank would be taken into the station for violating the terms of his restraining order.

When they went back to the bedroom upstairs, the room was silent and there on the inside of the window, lay the wasp, dead.

Horror Story

when the twilight
sleep ebbed
held fast to a slab
in Frankenstein's
laboratory of
alarming reason
I silently swore
to never write
of the horror

the gut tube
that looked like
a botched sex-change

Contribution

a presumptuous thing
a day out
of puberty
who's contribution
to the day
was coordinating
her scrubs
took your vitals
then asked if I believed
in god

you were floating
somewhere
between drugged
and dumbstruck
I was neck deep
between
Rod Sterling
and Edgar Allan

I may have
insulted her

naivety her
inappropriateness
her very presence
in my collapsed universe
but
she asked permission
to pray anyway

Room Number

when I asked you
why you didn't take
my call, you said
you don't like
phone calls, I know
that about you,
you said

I know, I said
I just want to hear
your voice

this isn't my
voice
you said

Blood Sugar Poem

at I short of
three hundred
I hit a wall
roadblocks
blockheads
insomnia
the metal snake
medallion
bouncing here
and there
off a lobster claw
marking me
inferior
infirmed
number conscience
every minute
every day
every night
and there's
no going back
no going on
without
the numbers
and
this poem
might make
it 300

There is a Power

Lone passenger in back of a white stre-tch limousine that is on fire.
Nobody is driving, the car cruises at a c r a w l
a downward spiral funneling into oblivion.
I look out the window with empty eye sockets.
The scenery changes, ruins of city
towering vegetation rising out of the disturbed earth
dwarfing every building like forgotten tombstones.
My lips, nose and ears fall away my face feels very thin.
I wither, crack, not even a husk,
only a pile of bone dust calcifying my clothes.
A man in a dark suit wearing a button that reads
'I LOVE MY FUCKING JOB'
waiting at the bottom of the d

       o

      w

       n

       g

        r

        a

        d

           e. He gets in back where I was seated and
pulls out a straw begins to snort my
remnants like an earthen cocaine.
The drip slides into his mouth
he spits what is left of me into the fire
surrounding death's baby carriage.

Matchstick, Acorn Hill

Some altered landscapes go unnoticed,
hidden by mature growth,
lush angular anomalies,
and streets continue on
as though limping was not a hindrance
only an eccentricity - limping slow
as our sun's heat is slow to reach the exoplanets
or slow as destined love can be before it is
fully embraced.

Self-definitions needing
to be re-defined and illusions
of future bliss needing
to be released for more authentic possibilities.
Years of pebble-hopping, fresh denials
embodied into lifestyles.
The spot is marked. Grass stained,
unwashable, obvious to everyone,

but you are on the rafters, singing
to a made-up ghost, you are whistling
the tune you learned as a child,
whistling without variation,
plodding the automatic path
you were told would to lead to joy,
to a mandatory means of fulfillment,

instead of seeing and serving the deformity,
blessing its merging waters with your own,
becoming stronger still, blooming as it grows,
methodically eliminating your most coveted
expectations.

Night is the Time

Night is the time for poetry
when acts by day
ease into silence
and dream
and there is the Dark, that knowing void
blanketing words,
time,
thought . . .
here is where we begin
Night, at the foot of the stairs
where poems have always been,
waiting.

The Skull

It sat in the Road
a Woman drove by.
She looked out the Window,
She saw it.
She pulled over.
She got out.
She walked
a little closer.
How strange, she said.
She did the Sensible thing
She called the Police
The Police arrived
The Chief said Thank You,
We'll take it
from here.
The Woman nodded
She was glad
to do her Part.
The Woman drove home.
She thought she'd pour a Drink
and go to bed
Early.
But when she opened the Door
it was on the entry Table.
What? the Woman sputtered.
That's not Right.
She turned away for a moment,
but when she looked back
it was still there.
Maybe if I ignore it, she thought
She went to the Kitchen
and grabbed a Glass
then she went
to the sitting Room
but when she opened
the liquor Cabinet
there it was.
I'll just go to bed now, the Woman said.
When she woke up
it was at the end of the Bed

facing her.
After a few Days of this, the Woman
had had enough.
She called the Chief
As she dialed
She thought she felt something
Watching her . . .
Sorry to bother you the Woman said
but I need to know something.
It's about why I called you
the first time—
Listen the Chief said
There's a lot
I could say.
I could give you a name, a past.
A whole lifetime
in five minutes.
You would know
almost everything;
the Dreams, the Hopes, the Aspirations.
And I could give you the End, too.
But listen.
Really listen.
Things happen.
All the time.
Sometimes you just have
to Let Go.
The woman understood.
She hung up.
She didn't say goodbye.
She Let Go.
The next morning
she woke up
alone.

The Taggers

He's out all night, my little brother, heedless, sometimes running with the pack, sometimes alone. My mother's child. I know what he is doing, chewing mushrooms and vomiting in the arroyo and worse, I suspect, climbing up the ridge of rocks that used to be fire, the backbone of a great beast fallen from the sky or risen out of the earth.

It's towards the end of summer, when cars fall in the sky, particularly in the dark hours towards morning when there is no moon.

And I tell him—baby brother, you may be almost a man and our mother may be too busy weaving a headband for that someone new who she likes but I see you…I know.

Sister, he says, child of our mother. Come on with me.

I don't like to climb the stone dyke. I never have. But it isn't difficult, or too far.

Aren't you afraid, I say. There are gangs out here, out from the basin land. They'd as soon roast your thighbone and eat the marrow as say hello.

He laughs.People of the basin aren't any tougher than people of the river. Come on, tough girl, river woman. Climb.

He lends me a hand, and lends it again. Up at the top, I can see rocks loom, slightly lit by the stars. He's brought a stick glowing out of the firepit and blows it into flame.

Light leaps up, and so does a herd of horned sheep, a bison, a long legged water bird. Painted on rock.

You! I say, touching it. It's beautiful, webbed feet, long bill, careful feathers.

It's one of his names, too. Private but not secret.

Aah…I breathe in. This is special, seen in a dream.

I see a naked woman, her form carved and chipped on the rock. Even headless, I know who she is, a little younger tan me, a little older than him.

Hey, I say, and turn to tease him, but his face has clouds in it and I stop. This isn't for teasing.

Follow me, he says.

On the other side of the rock is a nice smooth blank space. His stash is up here—a pouch, dried mushrooms, sticks, a few old pots of red ochre.

Child of my mother, he tells me. Put up your hand. Spread those long fingers. Beautiful. He paints around my hand with ochre.

I love him. He's my favorite person. This is the end of something, though. He loves others—a naked headless girl who in life swings her long braid, the gang he grew up with who now think they are men, the enemy coming for him, the animals he'll kill…In this, he is like everyone else.

But the paintings, the waterbird, that is different.

I don't want to stop. I put up my other hand, too. Surround it in red paint. Leave a print on the rock. Forever.

I was here.

More stars fall out of the sky in the quadrant toward the mountains. Soon light will creep out of the basin land and up over the river and it will be morning.

Soldier

He is a soldier, but he doesn't want to fight.
He wants to sell his weapons to buy her anklets instead.
He wants to melt his adrenaline for her adornment.

When fierce rage of winter bites his heart,
He desires for her soft bosoms for warmth.
He too wants to be a spectator of her beauty.

When his hands shake in an exchange of gunfire;
He remembers- how politicians laid their hands on her;
And how her beauty ravaged by powerful corporations.

He also remembers how greedy eyes turned her into half-dressed attires,
And now in some beauty contest she parades herself naked.
His blood flow reduces to nothing; and his cold soul torments

He tacitly agrees to gun fire, and surrenders to death.
He forgets about the deafening sounds of guns
He does not want to live anymore; he simply wants to die.

O life! I Love You

O life! Whenever you gave me wound,
And when I bled,
I just dripped and colored your canvas red.

Whenever I was blessed with sadness,
And when I cried,
I simply shed my tears to quench your thirst.

I never forgot you when I was happy,
And when I was glad,
I gave you a hug, and just smiled.

I was never ungrateful,
I enjoyed my festivals and failures with you,
And I gladly take your mischief and bore every grief.

Now, it is time to say good bye,
O life! I lack words, and don't know how-
To say: that I love you so much.

Death

The most terrible death is:
A death of a desire in a living body,
Where being desirous is-
The only sign of living.
When consumption stops, consumption of the body starts.
Without desire, human is not human.
He is dead or divine, perhaps.
But for sure, he is not living.

Contributors' Biographies

Allen Forrest is a graphic artist and painter. Born in Canada and bred in the U.S., he has created cover art and illustrations for literary publications and books. He is the winner of the Leslie Jacoby Honor for Art at San Jose State University's *Reed Magazine* and his Bel Red painting series is part of the Bellevue College Foundation's permanent art collection. Forrest's expressive drawing and painting style is a mix of avant-garde expressionism and post-Impressionist elements reminiscent of van Gogh, creating emotion on canvas.

Omar ZahZah is a Los Angeles based short story writer and poet, as well as a PhD student in Comparative Literature at UCLA. His work has appeared in such publications as *Vulcan: a literary dis-allusion, Poetic Diversity, The Chiron Review, The Horror Zine, RipRap*, and *Westwind.* Several of his poems were published in the collection Beside The City of Angels: An Anthology of Long Beach Poetry, released by World Parade Books.

Allison Grayhurst is a member of the League of Canadian Poets. She has over 500 poems published in international journals and anthologies. She has eleven published books of poetry and five collections, as well as six chapbooks and one e-chapbook. She lives in Toronto with her family. She also sculpts, working with clay; www.allisongrayhurst.com

Scott Thomas Outlar survived both the fire and the flood...now he dances with the waves of the Tao River, flowing and fluxing with the ever changing tide of life's existential nature. His words have appeared recently in venues such as *Dissident Voice, Novelmasters, Jotters United, Dead Snakes*, and *The Poetry Community*. His debut chapbook "A Black Wave Cometh" will be released in April through Dink Press. More of Scott's writing can be found on his blog at 17numa.wordpress.com.

David S. Pointer currently serves on the advisory panel at "Writing for Peace." David is also a new assistant poetry editor for "As You Were: The Military Review."

Felino A. Soriano is a poet documenting coöccurrences. His poetic language stems from exterior motivation of jazz music and the belief in language's unconstrained devotion to broaden understanding. His work has been nominated for the Pushcart Prize and Best of the Net anthologies. He lives in California with his wife and family and is a director of supported living and independent living programs providing supports to adults with developmental disabilities. Visit felinoasoriano.info for more information.

Dustin Pickering is founder of Transcendent Zero Press, a poetry publishing company that releases the quarterly *Harbinger Asylum*. He was a Special Guest Poet at Austin International Poetry Festival in 2013, and a feature at Public Poetry in the same year. He is published at *Seltzer online, Lost Coast Review, di-verse-city 2013,* and the Muse for Women anthology, among others.

Susan Beall Summers, Hutto, TX has been writing poetry from a young age. Her first collection of poetry, Friends, Sins & Possibilities was published in 2011 by DreamersThree Press. Currently she is a video journalist for Texas Nafas on Channel Austin. She is an active Austin poet, member of Austin Poets International, Austin Poetry Society, and Writer's League of Texas. She is also a ghostwriter and editor and recently helped create Cameo by Marcie Eanes. Her poems appear in *Ilya's Honey, Texas Poetry Calendar, Lifting the Sky: Southwestern Haiku and Haiga, Harbinger Asylum, Baylor's Beall House of Poetry, Small Canyons Anthology, Di-Verse-City,* and others. www.tidalpoolpoet.com

Wade Martin is co-editor of the *Texas Poetry Calendar*, co-host of the Mind Maze Reading Series for Raw Paw Press, and a 2014 Pushcart nominee. He is also a Teaching Artist with Badgerdog and The Freehand Arts Project. His work can be found in *Perfume River Poetry Review, Freshwater,* and *Haibun Today.*

Amitabh Vikramdwivedi is university faculty and assistant professor of linguistics at Shri Mata Vaishno Devi University, India; and author of two books on lesser known Indian languages: A Grammar of Hadoti and A Grammar of Bhadarwahi. As a poet, he has published around fifty poems in different anthologies, journals, and magazines worldwide. Until recently, his poem "Mother" has included as a prologue to Motherhood and War: International Perspectives (Eds.), Palgrave Macmillan Press. 2014.

Jillian Cormier is about to graduate from university with a bachelor's degree in English Professional Writing. As a full-time college student, she is focusing her time on honing her writing skills and expressing her creativity through various media of drawing and painting. Since she was in elementary school she has explored the malleability of the written word in different forms of poetry, short stories, and novellas. "Trapped" will be her first published short story. She enjoys writing fiction and fantasy on her free time and lives a quiet life with her family in New England.

Miriam Sagan blogs at Miriam's Well (http://miriamswell.wordpress.com). She is the author of 25 books, including the recent collection from Sherman Asher, SEVEN PLACES IN AMERICA: A Poetic Sojourn. Recently won New Mexico Literary Arts Gratitude Award in Poetry, and has received the Santa Fe Mayor's Award for Excellence in the Arts. Sagan also does text and grassroots installations--most recently at Salem Art Works and at The Betsy Hotel.

Kayla Volpe is a twenty-something spoken word artist originally from Middletown, New York. As a young poet, Volpe attended and competed in the Woman of the World Poetry Slam in Austin, Texas in 2014, as well as the National Poetry Slam in Cambridge, Massachusetts in 2013. Her first self-published chapbook, "Establishing Sovereignty" was released in February, 2014 and included a collection of bildungsroman-esque poetry. She studies Creative Writing as an undergraduate at Binghamton University and currently performs for audiences locally, and regionally.

Wanda Morrow Clevenger lives in Hettick, IL – population 200, give or take. She's widely published with over 300 pieces of work in 114 print and online publications. A full-length poetry manuscript is currently stalking unsuspecting presses.

Parker Weston is a multimedia artist residing in Mesa, Arizona (voted the most conservative big city in the United States) mainly focused on assemblage/sculpture. He has a comic strip, Animation Taxidermy, several short animations and musical project Stembreo, to boot. When he was a child, an overpaid psychic told his mother that he would be a writer someday. He was relieved later that she was spared the news that along the way he would be an adult shop janitor and backpacking drifter before this writing business ever came into effect.

M. R. Briceño is a young writer from León, México. A slacker and a procrastinator, he wastes his time writing instead of studying."

Nothing. No One. Nowhere. Vol. I No. 5

Edited by Sonnet Mondal
Featuring: Vihang A. Naik, Eugenia
Tan, David S. Pointer, Dr. Bina
Biswas, Matthew Wilson, James
Robinson, Zinia Mitra, Dr. Arvind
Nawale, Prshant Mothe, Dr.
Shamenz

Nothing. No One.
Nowhere. Vol. I No. 4

eaturing: Kanchan Chatterjee, Billy
rfosh, Dr. Mary Annie A.V.,
om Kafley, Douglas G. Campbell,
zal Moolla, David S. Pointer,
ristopher Barnes, Matt DiSparti,
chelle Gilsdorf, Raud Kennedy,
dama Chandra Panigrahi, Catori
miento,

More Poetry Titles Available from Virgogray Press

NO FEAR by Doctori Sadisco
In the Broken Things by Gillian Prew
Vegas Implosions by Chris D'Errico
By the Banks of the Ajoy, Jaideb Vanishes into the Blue by Subhankar Das
Elektra's Mouth by Suzi Kaplan Olmsted
Elephants I Didn't Ride by Peter Marti
You Are Not a Normal Human Being by Justin Blackburn
Sinister Splashplay by David S. Pointer
Ministry of Kybosh by Chris D'Errico
The End of Mythology by A. Molotkov & John S. Williams
Carcinogenic Poetry Anthology Volume 1-2
Beneath Our Feet by Mary Harrison
I Am South by Donna Snyder

www.ingramcontent.com/pod-product-compliance
Lightning Source LLC
Chambersburg PA
CBHW071350130626
46556CB00005B/2109